The Illuminations

The Illuminations

Poems by Mary Kay Rummel

Cherry Grove Collections

To Mary Ann and Gene
two adventurous
Readers - thank you
for your encouragement

Love,
Mary Kay

Published by Cherry Grove Collections
P.O. Box 541106
Cincinnati, OH 45254-1106

Typeset in Iowan Old Style by WordTech
Communications LLC, Cincinnati, OH

ISBN: 193345637X
LCCN: 2006930707

Poetry Editor: Kevin Walzer
Business Editor: Lori Jareo

Visit us on the web at www.cherry-grove.com

Acknowledgements

Cover Artist, *Blue: Departing*: Colleen McCallion
Book Design: Sandra Rummel
Author photo: Steven Wewerka

Thank you to all the editors/artists who published or performed my poems, sometimes in other versions.

ArtLife: "Forgetting the Rules," "Pilgrim," "The Scribe Daydreams," "Legend," "Fox," "A Long Marriage," "The Name of Destination," "Looking for the Chanting Monks"
California Quarterly: "From There to Here"
Comstock Review: "An Old Melody"
Luna: "Family Stories"
Main Channel Voices: "Estuary"
Nimrod: "In the Margins—A poem sequence," "Histories"
Northeast: "Ragged Photograph," "Legend," "The World a Folding Book"
Qualitative Studies in Education: "Of That Country the Tongue"
Sidewalks: "Siena Beneath Me," "Making Form," "Pilgrim"
Sidewalks online: "Like Nothing, Then Something"
Water-Stone Review: "In the Middle"

The Talking of Hands, New Rivers Press.: "Elegy"
33 Minnesota Poets, Nodin Press: "Burgundy Trillium"
Between Stone and Flesh, anthology of 2002 Lake Superior Writers' Contest: "Cairns," "This is How She Will

Not," Hartland Point" (these poems were included
in a dance performance choreographed by Lisa
McKhann in Duluth, MN)
LondonArt Exhibition Catalogue: "Legend," "Closer to
Flame"(these poems were chosen by Andrew
Motion to be exhibited at London/Art)
"Of That Country the Tongue" and "In the Middle"
were reprinted in *Becoming a Teacher in the New
Society* edited by Mary Kay Rummel and Elizabeth
Quintero and published by Peter Lang
International.
"In the Margins: A Poem Sequence" was performed
with musicians Gwen Perun and Prill McAfee in
Duluth and Minneapolis MN.

Thank you to those who helped make this book possible:

Colleen McCallion for the beautiful cover pastel and Sandra Rummel for her cover design;

David Mason, Patricia Barone and Roseann Lloyd for their help with this manuscript;

the members of Onionskin who have given me feedback on these poems over the years, especially Sharon Chmielarz, Kate Dayton, Carol Masters, Patricia Barone, Nancy Raeburn, Tom Heie and Diane Jarvi;

also Elizabeth Quintero;

Kevin Walzer and Lori Jareo of WordTech Communications for their dedication to bringing this book and other books of poetry into the world;

Liza Fourré and Roseann Lloyd of Art Workshops in Guatemala, Joan Drury of Norcroft; Robert Hedin of The Anderson House, and the artists' community of Vermont Studio Center;

Joe Cardella, Phil Taggart, Jackson Wheeler and Roe Estep in Ventura County, CA for opportunities to publish and read these poems;

Tim, Timothy and Andrew for their constant encouragement.

For Mari Ella

Contents

The continuous process of remaining open and accepting of what may reveal itself through hand and heart on a crafted page is the closest I have ever come to God.

Donald Jackson
Illuminator and calligrapher
St. John's Illuminated Bible

In the Margins of the Pages

Inspired by the *Book of Kells*, Trinity College,
Dublin

Of ink of the green-skinned holly
My little dripping pen travels
Across the plain of shining books

from an 11th century poem in honor of St. Columcille

Illumination

It is March 19, feast of St. Joseph;
the *Book of Kells* is open to St. John.
His eyes, bottomless, now blue, now green
(pigment of lapis lazuli from Afghanistan)
engulf me, as when I walked into the Mormon Center
in Salt Lake City, saw that giant Jesus on the ceiling.
I wanted to fall face to the floor,
wanted to believe it all,
The whole creed of it. The repent and follow of it.
The flesh and blood and bread of it.
I do and its opposite. Like that Celtic painter
in the tower, I hold in my mind two thinks at a time.

The lion god on every page
reviver of cubs, swallower of sinners:
we with our heads in its mouth.

God is in the Scribblings

Kells Monastery, 800 A.D.

Summer Winter
the monk writes
in a stone tower
that shuts out both Viking
and rain-washed air.

He transcribes holy words
onto calfskin—it's the doodling
that keeps him going.
His pagan hand draws wildly
in colors he creates

painting lizards kermes from
the bodies of pregnant insects
giving 'A' a crown of gold
filling the curve of 'J'
with birds colored from verdigris,
folium, woad.

(Not gold, really
yellow as in Christ's celtic hair
from arsenic sulphide
toxic for artists.)

He remakes the heaven he was told.
In his mind stories take sides,

dogs snarl at the cross, mice eat
sacred bread, the snake is watching
limbs of men and women twine.

It's slow at first
if a smell, the dark root
if a shape, running
if a taste, being there
if a love, finding something
if a body, beneath.

Recipe for the Scribe

Ink for the apprentice

Mix soot gum liquid
cuttlefish and lamp black
soak oak apples and mix with
liquid flour, copper crystals.

Parchment

Made from sheep or goatskin
vellum from skins
of young animals—
soak them in stream water
running for days
immerse in still waters, lime
for a fortnight
scrape off hair and soak
for weeks
rinse, stretch, dry in the sun
polish with pumice
whiten with chalk
dress with oil
cut into sheets.

Also in the margins

While the illuminator paints
his sexy dreams,
the scribe complains
about bad conditions
cold, poor light, writes,
"Reader, do not find fault
with the script for my arm
is cramped through excess of labor.
My stomach is empty,
my hand shakes."

This too.

The Animal Lessons

If you could see the moment
you fuse with what you aren't,
your beginning, your end,
if you could look down on that
cacophony of crows with
the concentration of an owl
eyes rimmed yellow
you think you would understand
that in the world you see
every thing means something else.

Peacock

I know this bird, have seen the grail
      where a dreaming monk wove
            human bodies with peacock.
                  Flesh so hard it never putrefies.
            So I lift weights and walk
trying to harden flesh and bone
to stop that soft sinking.

Oh I have heard the wave wings make
      when they move, maybe prayers as once
            was thought, maybe an angel igniting
                  a poem, granite and leap into flight.
            Make us human and peacock
      grant us limestone and minnow
feathers and hand.

Snake

They didn't know what to do with her
those christian-pagan men
so they made her snake.
She curls
all over
        their pages
               shedding her skins
                      always returning.
They named her Christ
in his resurrected body.
        They called her
               the source of all sin, entangled her
among the letters
        of this gospel then drew
               her head in the lion's mouth.

She's that thing within the thing
that changes but does not change.

Once I stepped off a trail
        while hiking the coast path

trying to shortcut to another hill
        and disturbed a nest of snakes.

The scattershot sprayed.
        I jumped back to the path and stayed

thinking of them there.
        She's that kind of knowing.

Unicorn

Tapestry—A mon seul désir

Let me live in love again
object of my desiring
with the one who loves my
heavy sweetness, my yes
object of my desiring.

Let my heart be feral
to my own desire
my days are a river
my nights discalced.

How fast this
holy terrain
of my wanting.

Ecotone

Zone where species blend

This moment
    this breath
    this time—
        this is what there is.

This serpent
    this wing
    this red pool eye–
        this is what is next.

 This bone
    this boat
    this beak—
        one's become the other
        this is what will be.

And you on this millefleured earth
that sailed, will be sailing
this illumined eye—

this is what you have.

She Who Cannot Be Dissected

Her face flies apart
when you look, scatters
like starlings from a tree
then reassembles new.

That's how I see her when
Trinity College Library
displays a model made by
a Renaissance doctor—
a pregnant woman
belly cut away showing
the child inside her
with a man's face—

set between the rows of marble busts
(Newton & Plato & Aristotle &
Hamilton & Demosthenes & Locke.)

> *Not the calices on the mountain*
> *not the cloud it wears*
> *not the split in the stone*
> *not the new frond*
> *not the ear of the birch*
> *not the footsteps of wine*
> *not the vagina, not the beech*
> *see her grip the earth*
> *see her feet, her feet.*

Around the Edges of the Pages, Curves And Coils

1

Trinity knots and celtic coils
women like the interlaced foliage
a face caught there, the face of an owl.

2

At the Glastonbury well
a woman bends to fill her jars
with water that flows
from spring to well to spigot—
a lion's mouth.

From the lion's mouth
the water flows
into bowls that look
like uterus, fruit halves
through a labial opening
to more bowls
beneath and beneath
then onto a flower
or phallus then
into a garden pool.

Her smile dazzles in her dark face.
I drink and wash.
Mother, I want to say, I'm ready now.

3

Is that what this illumination is?
Like water, that and not.

4

Walking in the woods, I saw
birches looping and bending
and more than birch,
around one tree, a numinous
light that my eyes missed
in their brief soundings.
And so are we, ourselves and more.

5

Let me touch you Lady.
You are in the margins of the pages,
and so am I.

Beginnings

It happens as you drive. Ahead the mountain
in all its spring stages—low band of trembling green
the brown weave of branches not yet budding
the always pine, the shift and tilt of stony light.
Your whole life is the brown late greening part
stones shaped from your own dreaming
from the chorus of voices that come whispering there
and you have to write the book of your own hours.

This Illumined Eye

Histories

Give me writing I can take
as evidence of the world's love,

A letter, a bill, a diary,
scribbled notes I call history.

The birthday card from my mother
addressed to the best of daughters,

given to me just before she died, words
I waited too long to hear, to see.

When I read my mother's writing
I hear her, see her hand shaking.

I am my own collector, docent
telling my survival, my subject,

the past looms while the future
shrinks on parchment scraps.

Give me books I can see and hear
at the same time:

the Rabula gospels, the Lindisfarne,
a copy of the Qur'an, a Buddhist folding book.

Let me read the way a child
reads a picture book,

a kind of eating
urging me to utterance,

a reading of the body,
the holy words, the world.

Of That Country the Tongue

Years and years ago these sounds took sides.
—Seamus Heaney

The waters of Bath wear the face of the goddess
Latin Minerva,
       Celtic Sulis,
            the Gorgon Medusa
                    each alphabetic snake `
                    uncurled
yet headphones translate Latin inscriptions
and those words are male to me
language of
      priests,
            male choirs,
                    cathedrals.

I was a child among its roots and syllables
repeating what I didn't understand
      ave
            magnificat
                    anima mea dominum.
I remember the voices as one singing, but

left too soon the Irish of my grandmother,
harsh gutturals of West Seventh street,
and English novels of my mother
to enter the silence of my father
and the Latin conjugations I was taught
belonged to God.

History's a mind that's never still
       with its black thoughts–ravens,
            its white thoughts–gulls,
                     not blends, but digraphs
tossing and cawing among great ruins.

Looking for the Chanting Monks

Shrewsbury, England

A learning to live in a ghosted now.

The journey marked by towns grimy
      with industry and grey

sky, tree lined cloister walks,
      church to graveyard where centuries

are thrown together, black stones
      in an unbraced earth, leaning like teeth.

I dream the sides of the tracks are lined
      with those who have lived before.

How can we travel anywhere without
      acknowledging those we pass?

Family Stories in London

An Exhibition of Greek Icons

After the spring equinox the sun rising low in the south
shines like a laser through spaces in locust and oak
strange lights in a burnished city climbing steps
golden, flecked like those Byzantine icons,
the black architecture visible but not diminishing,
an exhibit of light, *A Conversation With God.*

home

I came carrying stories from the Bangladeshi waiter
in the Afghan restaurant across Marylebone street.
He poured free glasses of wine and thick coffee
and talked of his move to London, now home, how
his parents came for work, want to return, but
stay to be near their grandchildren, how
his wife just arrived, wants to go back to her family.

uneasy

In one icon, the Virgin Hodegetria holds a baby with
a man's face. In another, Mary turns away from the child,
Joseph broods with rounded back, angels love each other,
only ox breath keeps the child warm and the flecked gold
reveals the dark and brindled god beneath.

away from

When I hiked Bodmin Moor with my brother
we found stone circles beneath Rough Tor
mostly buried, where families gripped life
in the endless rain the way ours took root
on West Seventh as the city grew around us.

Streetcars changed to buses. Tail fins
filled our yard and talk of cars, the small house
where we moved away from each other—
he, to the earth's cold edges, Siberia, Alaska,
me, to books, icons, babies.

In the old photo we are toddlers
sitting in front of a garden.
I am teaching him to read
and he looks beyond me
towards the hills and river.

making new

I studied icons and thought of hands
that made them, great forces concentrated there.
Did the holy man fall in love with the woman
as he painted? At night did he dream of holding her?
Breathless by morning making his way after Mass
to his desk, did he take brush in hand to touch her
mouth, hips, beneath the folds her breasts,
bowing his head in prayer   desire   painting?

each equinox

In our turnings we are chased by this light.
It burns through our small stories
to the great ones, and we are changed.

Ragged Photo

Silence is and is not the end of Mahler's adagietto.
The lake heaves with waves from a freighter, invisible.
It is possible to be with someone who is gone.

Many days I forget you the way I forget the winter lake
hidden from me beneath clouds of steam, or I am hidden
from it, in my warm car, veiled with fatigue.

I refuse to acknowledge that cold place
where you are with the girl I was,
our names carved on an empty bench.

Inishmore

Aran Islands, Ireland

1

My eyes scan silhouettes of dry stone walls
that crown the ridge, clear sky visible through
their holes, as they wind fort-ward where tourists
claim the path, the young so young here where
monastic stones endure and *waves crash in ebb*
and flow to number countless bones. I want
to stay till dark, *each thought a linnet dipping*
toward its own night roost as urban students'

backpacks slide toward cliffs where humans
walked eight thousand years or more.
The wrinkled old seem older here, presences
not wanting to exit the brambles and ditches
the always crunch of foot on stone where suffering
built these hopeless fields from seaweed, sand.

2

The sea takes chunks of cliff below Dun Aengus,
eating it the way that seals take bites from salmon
as they swim. The fisherman said, "Still, they'll jail
you in Ireland longer for killing a seal than a person.
I don't want to fish for salmon anymore, too hard
that life. It's always been too hard here
on this island. When a baby stuck feet first
they rowed the screaming mother across

that sea to the mainland, it storming more than not.
There's work here now that tourists come; we bring
our children home." In the ruins rock reflects the sun,
warming seals and tourists. A great blue heron
fishes below the pier, then flies down the beach
to become another grey stone tossed on an Irish shore.

3

She stands alone under stars, within the coruscating
universe, inside the ancient walls, climbs the raised
central stone. Facing west, she intuits the meaning
of this ruin of iron age, of bronze age, this most
westward spot in Europe. She is part of those who
stumbled up the path in the dark, who worshipped
here, part of the rock itself, part of those born from
rock, those who stomped or brushed across it,

part of those who went back in. She feels weightier
than granite eggs thrown on shore by ice age glaciers,
older too. She thinks she is learning at last to trust
the energy of things, to wait and feel the earth's tug
as it swings around to carry all before it, loving
that force. She stares out at all there is.

Cairns

Inverness, Scotland

1

The loch is slate air, peat smoke and mist.
We find in the field among cows and sheep
the stone age graves flanked by standing stones.
No one really knows who the Picts were
or what's in these graves appeasing their gods.

2

I set up the tripod and camera
comforted by its whir and dream myself back.
At first only the sound of sheep bells distracts
a bleat, a moo, the feeling of being among

until a couple and their two children
arrive, talking as they find the ancient
doorways, stone beds, barn and byre.

Both scientists, they know the whys
of stone. What I hear is hidden between.
The parents' eyes are flint.

3

The stones tell only different ways of seeing:
say all is relationship, everything counts
in blank fields, hovering on the edge of sense.
Possibilities make their own light,
scraps of touch, touching
behind them, a hand wavers.

4

Echoes spin round me, wind-riven.
When you sink into such a place
death could come upon you the way
it came to the old Scottish woman
who was resting on a rock in her field.

Death made her part of the field
of the run-on sentence of snow,
the afterthought whispers of flake.

5

*Underneath my life is a life
I have chosen not to live.*

Adumbrare on water, in air
between stone and flesh
between fragment and completion
between trace and memory
distance so great it is not.

An Old Melody

Highland man steps slow
round the stone circle
round the Loch
slow and quiet
dark so near
the song he plays
lifting my hair.
It rises and rises
over the bare hills
tearing at my heart
the piper marching there
with the tune leaping up
the moor and echoing
a memory of
monastery bells
buried beneath the sea.
Frahnk warns a heron
on the wild distressed shore
the long necked women wail.

Hartland Point

Poem for two voices

Who are those that fly   *after listening*
                                to Beethoven's Ninth
                                I step

like cloud
                                into city light

enter into rock
                                a clarity in
                                the sideways
                                slant

become salt
                                in the brain

become thunder
                                a sudden seeing

stricken
                                it's like that

waterfall in one ear
                                inside

surf in the other
                                outside

oil of gladness
mantle of praise

                        the same

spirit riding

                        I have been

the body

                        wanting (this)

                        lightning

knocked to the ground

                        a transformation

by wanting

                            what is

happy with campion

                        far

rock

                        to be

tide pool clamor

                        near

feasts   feasts
all senses like tentacles

                        closer than I thought.

Pilgrim

1

In his studio the artist
painted shell after shell,
a series, red of persimmons
and rubies purple limned.
He painted a shell like
the stage Botticelli made
for Venus, a begging bowl
shell that pilgrims
wear around their necks
to Santiago de Compostela.
One glittery like the paua
shell that landed at my feet
on the wild south beach,
shell become ear listening to sea.

Then he began painting ears
layered white mushrooms
lined in red and black
bulbous, they got larger
until they left the canvas.
He sculpted an ear
and attached it to a birch
in the orange part beneath
the peeling bark.
The ear hanging there
seemed part of the birch
listening to itself.

2

A woman went deep
into the arctic looking
for silence to see what it was
and heard herself in her
empty ears. In a land where fells
rise like waves from rock
she heard the sound one hears
at night in a quiet room:
a soft persistent whoosh
beneath the owl's wings
inside your ears or brain,
something or nothing at all.

Why, she wondered, was she still so lonely?

Burgundy Trillium

The head hangs too heavy for its stalk

three petals curled back into redlined leaves
        reveal the acidic furred, acidic yellow center

the stem springs from three lower leaves
        a storyteller's dream

           *

a woman walking picked one:
she pulled one petal and a child appeared with a question
she pulled another and a young woman appeared, an answer
pulled the last and an old woman came just in time

not related to *tripalium,* the Roman torture tool
that gave birth to travail and from that travel—
no, that's another story

trillium, related to trio, the clovered trinity
to trill, warbling and wind gashed
and to the wine red of unicorn tapestries

           *

 a trinity of women there
        one sews
                one looks in a mirror
                        one puts away her jewels
all the same woman

Making Form

On looking for "Les Très Riches Heures
du Duc de Berry"

At Cluny, though she searched for a great copy,
the Hours were dull as if the blood
used to paint them (the way barns were painted
with milk and blood of cows) had dried
burgundy burnt down, greens mulched.

> *There were no Hours*
> *beneath the Hours*
> *trees but not shadows*
> *water but no cities beneath*
> *no long brushes of deep violet*
> *women were never trees*
> *the owl, no owl.*

She'd rather live with memory
ruddy as the real, the rose
that died blooming inside her.

She touches the lake, fingers licking
its black pelt, sees dried berries,
ragged asters those velvet ribbons,
knows the signs of coming cold, imagines
men bending over the vines, women
putting wine on the table, remembers

till her thoughts grow spare, a man and a woman
standing naked in a room filled by light so pure
it thins the shadows on their bodies.

Translations

Lovers look into water never thinking of Polycrates
who threw a ring into a river for good luck
and the god sent it back in the mouth of a fish.

*

A Parisian illuminator painted
Boccaccio's tale but confused
the Italian *anello* with *agnello*
and made a fish with a lamb
in its mouth appear as the Persians
hung Polycrates.

Was it a failure of translation then,
or a failure of meaning?
Either way, Polycrates was killed.
Did he betray himself, believing
in symbols that didn't work?

Take the letters carved
on a stone tablet that I touched
in that small museum at Epidaurus.

The spiral Mycenaean script could be
a record of business or judgment or irony
the story of a murder by twins, how one
was punished and one went free.
Maybe I touched six goats with bells
or two donkeys nuzzling.

The spiral script could be a love poem,
words that come close to what they mean, could
say love smells of oregano, is an owl in the night, says
love gives six gold coins, a bolt of filtered cloth,
is luck, is lapis, basil, a fish with a lamb in its mouth.

Learning in Normandy

Avranches, France

In a small town in Normandy I visit an old monastery
with winding stone steps, glass cases of manuscripts
kept in damp dark. Then, I walk out
into light, to a square bursting with life.

It is first communion Sunday for girls posing
in long lace, for boys shining in white suits,
for mothers with camera smiles, fathers with
minds on the coming dinner and wine.
In a place where everything moves upward
or down to the flat tide bed, I listen to a language
I know little of, glimpse what I've lost, what
I never had. Their lives like mine, I read
their hungers, their guilts, their overdrafts.
Their Sundays don't hurt. I know their happiness
the way sometimes in a museum the iconic eyes
of some saint look into mine and irony lifts
from my brain. What's left is recognition.

I walk downhill with it,
able to name some of the parts but not the whole,
inside me, what I know.

Visible in Air and Water

Le Mont–Saint–Michel

Because nature was too beautiful
        monks built these walls

because the tide bed is so wide
        quicksand swallowed pilgrims

when a woman gave birth on it
        the child was promised to god

the way a young monk vows stability
        I move on

when the fields needed fire
        poppies came, then war

Closer to Flame

Viewing the stained glass windows
at La Sainte-Chapelle

This red illumines
grains of sand,
the moment burns
from inside out.

An osprey guts a fish
as she watches the canal
the cochineal sound
wholly the osprey's.

She's taken more than
halfway by the smells:
trillium releasing vermillion,
fiddlehead ferns, wet tongues

and by the sounds: echo blue,
blood chilling the night she
hears wolves howl, cries swirling
the bowl of the bay, and by Monet's

last lilies, Chartres blue nymphs,
or the year he died, Renoir's
bathers, breasts glowing,
their stunned, celestial veins.

Siena Beneath Me

A grey cat leaves a recessed doorway
glides over stone that cools
in moonlight beneath the campanile

deserted Siena square, stone benches
burning bush, acacia
all black shadows on white

left over echo of motorbike
rumbles beneath it all

        a violence on the floor of the Duomo
        the mosaic, "Slaughter of the Innocents"
        those babies looking so real
        were real, are real

        driving away and suddenly seeing
        in the rear view mirror the whole bulk
        of the black and white striped cathedral

        St. Catherine's skull saved in a gold reliquary

the large and frightening trapped
for a moment in the small

Holy Saturday in Siena

Is this always a feast day of spring rain?
Rain on brown red stone still warm
rain in canyons between stone walls
rain through echoes of motorbikes, voices,
rain sending people running from the Campo.

Rain slashing thoughts

When smoke rises from the swinging censer
it rises on blue waves from vault to vault
in the nave's ceiling, blue waves of belief
rain down on us
rain trance
transcend
transcendence
belief, a word I can barely write.

Rain slashing sentences

Words no longer pour from me
but wrap me round
as the rain on long afternoons
the losing rain
too light to hold it rain.

Rain slashing time

There is a journey where the hero child
returns to the land of her mother's belief
hands and knees rain
on the steps to the shrine
more water than stone.

The World A Folding Book

Voices

Are not forever but travel centuries
strung across stone, skin, paper,
a tablet carved in three languages.

A poet through her long brush strokes
can hear that rain, understand that it fell
all night on the bamboo roof of the boat.

The night a palpable thing, rain insulates
the morning, tears leaves from the trees,
brings down the not-yet-fallen.

After, soft holes in the silence, smell of cinnamon.

On the Way to Chiang Rai

Thailand

Maybe she recognizes my own
kind of wandering, the Lisu elder

who smiles at me, a smile from
one older woman to another.

This small plane is the hand that plucks
me up and carries me to another place.

Below us the rice fields reflect sun
then we are over green mountains.

From China through Burma the Lisu
traveled to those mountains,

dreamscapes with string roads
and roosters crowing.

She is with her two adult children—
a mother light simmers in her brown eyes.

My roots hang like an orchid's in air.

In Xian

China

The screech of the train whistle in the night,
a scream in the Muslim bazaar. I am
in Xian, air thick and acrid, taxis weave
smells of sesame oil, coriander and

the police drag a young man from a courtyard.
His mother rides on the boy's back, howling.
Angry muttering men follow.

Everyone stops for a few minutes to watch,
a freeze frame, then everything moves again:

crickets, birds in straw cages sing;
a woman rides a bicycle, pole across
her shoulders, a roasted duck skewered
on each end; a man balances a long
rolled carpet on his handlebars.

I am standing in this world, knowing
it is not a movie. In the silence
between train whistles, I wonder
what comes next and next and after that.

The Name of Destination

On flying with two hundred Hmong people
migrating from a refugee camp in Thailand

If the edge has a look, this is it.

The grandmother who can't sit still
opens a plastic bag filled with food,
passes it to young men and women
who hold babies in embroidered carriers,
on their chests and on their backs.

Nameless, wearing only the name of their destination
printed on white tags, they remind me
of how my great grandparents held their children
in steerage bunks on a heaving ship out of Ireland.
Eyes dark rings, cheeks sunken, exhausted.

If jumping off happens, it is here.

After landing, a Hmong grandfather fingers
his bundle as he waits at the top of the ramp
for his family, brown eyes flickering.
He's wearing pink flip flops into a cold night
where fatigue, where snow, wind and maybe
a new history waits.

The Hmong hill people buried the placenta
in the place where a child was born hoping
to bring her back at the end.

If edge has a history, this is it.

Forgetting Home

As we walk, the road along the river
disappears into the hills, rain heavy.

Dragonflies, huge clouds of them, feed
on mosquitoes at dusk like the swarms

of red dragonflies in my yard last autumn,
still heavy with sex, just lifted by wind

not flying the females' stubborn flight
before egg laying, death.

So the mind floats out on the wind
then snaps back to now, to Chiang Rai

where I drift in lush teak and locusts
along the red-brown Mekok high and fast

sculpted mountains, orchids feeding on air
light deep, intense and creamy under clouds.

My thoughts unfold like nesting boxes
until I can't remember day or year.

Monasteries Around Every Corner

Chiang Mai, Thailand

The temple bells are bronze.

They swing and sing in the air
bells from forty-five golden temples pealing
over the noisy city on the edge of lush mountains
over the baldheaded nun who sits at the foot
of the Buddha and keeps the temple
over the empty beer garden with the boy-girl show
over the men and women who set up their stalls
every afternoon, and take them down each midnight
over the little Hmong boy with one tooth who smiles
through the glass window of the internet cafe
over his mother who sits with other hill tribe women
selling belts and purses and table cloths
over the thirty-year old monkey
that sits on a shelf in the tiny grocery store
over the man who cares for him
over the woman who puts birds in small bamboo cages
that she carries to the temple courtyard, and visitors
pay to free so they can be caught again.

All of us held in the heart of that ringing.

Learning How to Visit

La Antigua, Guatemala

A traveler finds herself in a foreign city.
Bougainvilleas bloom, people unknown
walk the cobbled street slowly, maybe
fearful of history. Maybe red blossoms
fallen on the walks hold more than shadows
and bloodshed is not a story for museums.
It is hard to be just a tourist, just one
when history weighs as much as the sun
that is heavier than the sky and orange
and fuchsia open dark lands.

The day is warm, light explodes.
Of course she goes to La Fuenta
where, smiling carefully, Bonificia
tells her how she makes her weavings,
ceremonial tzute, carrying them
on her head nine kilometers
from Santa Maria de Jesus.
Para usted, ciento cinquenta,
she says and the traveler buys
the way that tourists always do
not even knowing this journey
is a class for beginners.

In the Middle

René the van driver teaches us some Spanish,
says, *La mitad la naranja,* meaning half an orange,
also meaning, my spouse, my other half.
He wants us to stop halfway between
Panajachel and Antigua to shop at Paulina's,
a trap for tourists where we buy serapes
that we will never wear in public but they bring us
the comfort of the sixties and we know
sweet René gets a cut from the sale.
"The blue is good for you," he tells me.
The orange he holds up for Suzanne.

> *Seeing the beauty, learning to see*
> *the world in which it lives*

*

My mother used to say,
"See how the other half lives,"
meaning those who are not poor.
Now, mother, I live in the other half
but I am finding it's no half
only the tiniest tip of the orange
and all the rest are poor.
I like having money.
Can you tell me how to live my life?

> *I am searching for "la mitad,"*
> *the middle ground of guilt*

*

At sixteen, I worked part time
at the dime store with Rosita
who worked full time in yard goods,
all day cutting and measuring cloth.
I went to her house to play cards
in the West Side neighborhood,
poorer than mine on Seventh Street.
Her husband swore in every sentence,
Jesus and Jesus and Jesus.

René is a teacher but
makes more driving
for tourists—one thousand
quetzals a month.
He's good at saying,
No es correcto,
gives us conjugations.
When I ask, "What is a llano?"
he thinks it is "yawn" and we
learn *yo bastizo, ella*
bosteze, nosotros bostezamos.

> *Seeking a way to be closer to the world*
> *and be less a part of it*

*

I wanted to be like Jesus, was
already poor, had nothing
to give away so joined the convent,
made a vow to own nothing.
Even the toothbrush was "ours."
We were given two habits to wear
but we were not hungry.

Poverty was the easiest vow.

Searching for "la mitad"
the middle ground of guilt

*

A gift to visit the home of Zoila,
a weaver in her Mayan village.
She shows us how to make tortillas
over the open fire and eat them hot and fresh.
When we walk up mountain with the girls
Lilian Maribel, Astri Sofilia and Arelisa,
they show us fields of squash, cilantro, beans.
We see farmers working on fields so steep
they are tied so they won't fall. Boys come down
the path with wood stacked high on their backs,
Buenas tardes, buenas tardes.
Later, the girls sit at Zoila's new table
and read to each other in the fading light.

Seeking a way to be closer to the world
and be less a part of it

*

When I was a young woman
I wanted to come to Guatemala
to teach in the mountains
in my black veil and heavy shoes.
When I left the convent I said
I'd never again wear those black shoes,
but here I am walking in my time,
"the last half," walking the cobbled streets
of La Antigua wearing nun shoes

on my sore feet, the learner not the teacher.
I am watching the hands of weavers,
trying to reach them as they move
red and orange across their looms.

Seeing the beauty, learning to see
the world in which it lives

Azotea

A Rising Wind

This is the year for lavender in Guatemala.
      Jacaranda blossoms like candles lit from inside
send the eye upward to cloud-drenched volcanoes,
      lavender woven through bougainvillea that stay
halfway between pink and purple, each blossom
      winking its single eye. Intending nothing, I look
the way a jacaranda might look over the square,
      seeing its own color repeated in weavings spread
by the fountain for sale.

The mothers of San Andreas Ixtapa raised money so
      their children could learn a trade. Each table mat
sewn by children who cannot hear or speak shows
      one of these petals printed against white as if
it were picked up from the square and kept there,
      kept and kept, small light against the dark,
sewn on wrought iron machines, one Singer, five made
      in China, lined up like birds on a wire,
quiet now, six machines for six children.

In my mind the Singer's bobbin chatters to the lavender
      dress with puffed sleeves held between my grandmother's
thick fingers, shadowed by her flying grey hair.
      She taught me words like pattern, treadle, warp. I learned
to oil the motor but never learned to sew.
      Grandmother sewed for me, her favorite, my cousins said.
Musha child she clucked as she worked, *Musha* because
      our names were Mary, because my mother was her first,

because I had four brothers and there I was—alone.
Musha child, can't you be still?

It is a lavender light, not Lent's purple, a lavender like
        the Mayan Mary wears in the church of San Francisco.
If she or my grandmother came to me in the thickest
        part of the night, woke me with a flashlight asking
What do you know? I would say nothing—I know
        nothing after so much history, so much work.
My grandmother's eyes dimmed with sewing.
        Each child takes a place mat to hem, holds it
by the edges as if it were a petal.

So much   so little   I know nothing
        except wandering and looking up
                        pulled by this rising wind of color.

Guatemalan Smoke

La Antigua, Guatemala

1

Everything moves upward in the life of this place,
morning clouds, roofs of red clay, voices of children
on their way to school, church bells ringing forty times
for forty days and nights of wandering, no desert here,
bougainvillea and wisteria, hopeful pigeons, their backs
shining like wet, oily streets.

I see a bouncing pick-up with mother and baby pigs
nuzzling each other. A cow and her calf bawl from behind
trees that line a field of herbs. The volcano stands alone in blue.

From the fields smoke rises and my eyes collect bits
of pomegranate and lavender, weaving the colors with sounds
of earth voices, the petrichor smell of rain on dry ground.

2

Air, thick with belief, rises on smoke from burning incense,
smoke that curls around stations and statues in the churches
of my childhood. Let it mix with smoke rising from the charcoal
fires of the Maya, candle smoke and tobacco. Let it rise
with the memory of those who believed. When a woman visits
the faith of her mother's mother, blessed shall she be.

3

Sometimes the air is a soft orange rind but not today.
Today clouds roil volcanoes, mountains hide from mountains.
Today children carry Jesus and his mother on barges
through streets purple with smoke. Boys dressed as Roman soldiers
march to dirges that roll over the city, notes from brass, from drums,
slow beat, slow step, slow until it becomes your heart beat
and desolation rises inside you, rises on the smoke from censers
swung by small boys, purple smoke that hides Jesus on the barge,
blankets men laboring under the barge, hides the volcano.
Smoke left over from centuries of death and prayer in these streets
rises up, meets smoke from the fields, volcano smoke descending.

4

Village flattened by earthquake rises again out of dirt and stone,
shreds of wrappers and cigarettes, plywood walls, billboard walls,
roofs of tin flap in the wind. Village black with smoke from fires
that burn all day in the courtyard of the shrine of Maximón, air thick
with charcoal, lighter fluid, incense where women and children
sit and breathe, eyes closed. Inside the shrine, Mayan people wait
along blackened walls to leave gifts of drink and cigars, food
for the dark god in his house, as people have always left gifts,
quotidian, for their deities. An outsider, I light candles for my loves,
watch smoke rise to Maximón, watch it fall.

5

I watch a woman walking through the fields up the mountain.
She follows a switchback path climbing in her huipil, indigo skirt,
up and up, past others who are farming. Her fields are small
and on top. She climbs in the slant of the setting sun. To my eyes she

is the spirit of the mountain in a haze of smoke, meeting the light
coming down.

6

You can feel the dusk spreading its loneliness everywhere.
Whatever it is in the violet light you know the earth
is shifting its weight. You feel the sun begin to doubt.
Shadows billow like folds in skirts and you walk untethered
as smoke going up meets smoke coming down.

Hunger Well

The hole from which we came isn't metaphysical.
The one to which we go is real.
                                    —Robert Creeley

I loved once—do you see where stone face meets stone face
        a shadow.
I learned to withdraw—see the open mouths in terra cotta heads.
Now I disobey and surrender—over there, perched on
the cemetery walls on top of Acoma mesa one by one,
each life, each face
        different.
They said gods were jealous but no, more like guardians, the way
the mouths are always open and spirit holes in the walls face all
        directions
for those who die away to come home through, home to where
sun and rock make spirits—the way of the gods a helix, a spiral, never
        straight.

                                    *

My hungry heart, I saw it on the monitor, alone with it
the doctor purposefully late, my heart inside outside the same
mouth opening closing opening again bird mouth sinkhole.

                                    *

There's a beneath that water makes, where we are now,
caves, sudden collapses, a path to find, it's not good to fill in
diversions being the normal run of things. When the earth
sinks man the lifeboats, like the sculptor I met building his ark

among Lutheran graves and stones that slide to marsh,
round heads on marble bases, one for him, one for his wife
and between, a smaller base holding two heads—a boy,
a young man. *For my son,* he says, as he clips and weeds.
He died two years ago, was only twenty, clips and weeds
and covers the always hole through which we and those
we love might go, do go.

Elegy

Sometimes a boat just slips from its mooring.
Night falls, a vagrant magpie perches
       in the rata grove.
Wind buffets the air. Rain pummels the ground
Soaking footpaths. Mud sinks the town.
Sometimes the rain pours your heart out.
Sometimes a boat just slips from its mooring.

Blue Moon: A Walk

Hartland, England
—After Adam Zagajewski

Shamrock Store open late
Springfield pots lined up
like cabbages

I am young or getting
rather old
carrying only stubborn
blood

doors ajar
notes of "Blue Moon" float
into the street

from the ancient church

You saw me standing
alone...

"Our song," he said,
What was his name?
in the high school gym

I am sixty years or
nothing
I could begin my life

or not mine
It could be easy

                              Without a dream in my
                              heart..

windows partway open

                              whitewashed walls still
                              warm

 dreaming

                              of plenitude

or not enough
ahead of

                              or behind.

Estuary

The little river that wound through sand, gone,
swallowed by sea, only one curve, small pool
behind it where fresh meets salt, the beach stones
gone, birds forced further in, the sun now melon
now scarlet, islands mist lost, hard to distinguish
rocks from gulls, ribbons of them skim across
lavender foam and there on what's left of beach
one figure hunches, or is it driftwood holding on
to this bit and there against the surf the river runs
its melody and here I stand against night coming on,
hunched against change in mango light, in avocado
evening, I want to cross. To stand in amazement.

Once while sitting in the dentist's chair
I decided to believe. They gave me
earphones for distraction and suddenly
Joe Carter was singing "Deep River," his voice
a river deep running through a bleak wild valley,
harmony sung by a Siberian choir.

Against the deepening, two herons along the shore
both straight and curved make me wish for a neck
that could fold its way out of pain. While ribbons
of pelicans straggle west two egrets, chalky in the dark,
guard the entrance to the river pool, Pacific blue
lavender of Guatemalan jade, holy stone of the Maya,
fresh water and salt, lavender stone and water.

My mouth pulled sideways like a gargoyle's
I decided to believe because of that music,

the young dentist going at my tooth and gums
against all evidence, against my resistance,
with hammers and scrapers, music, river,
what flows out, goes somewhere.

Like Nothing, Then Something

All of it moving
like searching for
thumbnail red frogs
in Costa Rica, poisonous
hearts of the rainforest
their high tattoo around us
pip pip   pip
we look but can't see.
A steady thirst
a sliver of whale
a moving fountain
a knowing there is more
in the sheen and scale
of silence beneath
as if the forces
down there as if
the black shadows
water spouts were not
what we see of everything
the tiniest sliver
like Easter.

Legend

Twin rocks face each other in the desert just east of Acoma,—
twins separated at birth find each other—between them shadow
even at high sun. That is the large story, Foucault be damned.
The small story could be us two souls on separate quests
who found each other, face each other now, the years behind,
in the narrow space between—a shadow, where our eyes
and voices meet, not easy to get a foothold in a place like that.
Unlike the yucca and its moth we could survive without
the other. Between us now we want the shadow shape truth is.
Omens everywhere come to us like strays—not the condor but
its shadow across pinion and stone. The sacred needs the body,
loves the body—it's required, the way story becomes all we have
of what was true, making us twin saints, a place for hawks to settle.

Run, Red Fox, Run Run!

A glimpse of fox this morning behind
the rain, a flash of fire in the grey.
I think oak leaves in fall, ginger, paprika,
fringe of white. The male geese stretch
their barrel necks and spit toward a bush
of tail that waves, then disappears.
When I returned from the hospital we held
each other stricken by the glimpse we'd had
of what's to come, the truth of where, of what
we are, the moment raw as a hungry fox.
If only we could run for it, knowing
how fire will out in the end.

A Long Marriage

Means sex takes a long time
and sometimes pleasure happens in the distance
like watching a symphony play with no sound
and you have to hear it in memory.
When it works there is surprise
new flavors served on the old oak table,
surprise in the flash of the inexplicable
the one fact of the imponderable.

A long marriage means more talk than sex
talk that takes a long time
the details of the day expected and longed for.
It means holding hands as if trying to keep each other
when friends are getting cancer and dying
and life plays like a sax in the distance
and you have to see the performer in memory
and you cling to the one slow fact of the inexplicable
as you float away with all you thought you knew.
A long marriage means living in the smell
of another as much as your own
and when you squeeze his shoulders you think yes
these are right, here, now an imponderable
one slow fact, his thin shoulders.

You dig through the long day of a marriage
archaeologists of surprise.
The empty clogs in the much–rained–on grass
become passage graves the mind can enter
graves with bowls or offerings
where light on the solstice comes through

a tiny slit in the chamber where you
hold each other and celebrate
the one slow fact of the inexplicable
in the loss of what you once knew.

There is rawness in the year of a long marriage
awareness of what lies outside the winnowing.
In the night you see not constellations
but stars—listen to one night bird break
sentences into words, hear the voice
of the inexplicable and name one by one
each good the other has done.

Between Stone and Flesh

On the quay, near the lighthouse
 in the square, in the cemetery
        on all our open-air stages,

Dazed by facts, things, words, the separate parts
 more than openings, senses awash.
        Last night the full moon, a red flag rising.

This morning doves coo
 through clamor of cicada, motor bikes,
        voices in the narrow walkways.

I am found and kept by the spirit of this filling,
 by lemons beneath my balcony,
        sugar donuts and croissants
                on the shelves across the lane.

The baker's been working since two a.m.
 Stonecutters started pounding very early and I am
        struck rigid like the baldheaded man who
                smokes at his gate and looks at the sea.

Restoration

Hydra, Greece

So bright we can only look at shadows
we climb rock and then

up steps made long ago
climb with purpose and slowly

both feet on a step each time
because they are so steep

climb to the deserted monastery
high on the mountain on Hydra

through terraced olive groves
past a rock shaped like a lamb

through a wall of cicada to dry grass
in a courtyard where two donkeys nuzzle

from there we look straight down
a single sailboat far below, sea shifts.

*

Then we meet Demetrius, landscape painter
and restorer of old monasteries
whose brother works for Spielberg.

He gives us thick Greek coffee and candy like
Turkish Delight but I don't say that and Tim

in his shorts gets a tour but I can't go inside—

I have no scarf and have carried no skirt.
The stone receives the sun's light and reflects it back
here light meets light and I am what is dark.

The Scribe

She copies the gospel
above the branches, in the tower.
She dreams into light
falling on the page.
The light shines through
the branches, draws her in
and she writes a story
beneath the story.

Making the light she follows it.
Underneath is more,
too much light to see
in the margins of the world.

She writes on calfskin
with a hard tipped brush,
in ink from the green
holly berry, her letters

like the scribbling of rain on the lake's
wide page, breaking off light,
breaking off from the breaking light.
She is following deeper, weary
inside a womb of rock, of rain.

Once she sat in sunlight
near a waterfall and once
she walked near the southern sea.
Her mind is moving into another story
the letters on the page follow.
This is her story now and hers the light.

This is How She Will Not

Talk about loss anymore
the shadow that makes leaves shine.
She will go to Jackson Square, watch women
parade in pastel dresses and filmy hats
drink chicory coffee in the garden
while a mime dressed as an angel
lifts announcing arms
and the psychics set up stalls
she will not enter.

                            *

In Vermont a man paints his porch
and sings as he paints
old melodies of love and (   )
(she will not say it)
follow her.
I've hungered for your touch
he sings into the day so fine
a long lonely time he moans
to clouds hiding the highest peaks.

                            *

At home she will not write of (   )
All night the window open
to the two sounds of the lake.
Church bells scour deserted streets
The lighthouse blinks on its rock.

*

Even in October she will not
when the solidity of things
bay   barge
consonants of truck on bridge
call back the ones she has (   )
when Superior churns them up, ragged
saying yes, you know us we're yours
then swallows them again
while gulls cry *mine, mine, mine.*

So much (   )
among us.

The World, a Folding Book

The pictures find me.
I don't need the rubricator
who wrote directions on top
of another scribe's work
telling others how to read it.

Sesame, cumin, oregano
smell of olive and lemon
small boats
with black motors
anchored off shore.

All running together
stone, red dirt
taste of peaches
heat lifting moisture
from my skin
everyness of cicada
texture of thalo blue
the ancient alkahest
connecting
things not words.

This stone ring around this lemon tree
we choose the things we love the way
the child draws
what is most loved larger
at the bottom of the page.

Notes

The quotation that introduces this book is from Donald Jackson, the renowned calligrapher and illuminator of the St. John's Bible, the only handwritten and illuminated Bible commissioned since the advent of printed books more than five hundred years ago. St. John's Abbey and University in Collegeville, Minnesota commissioned this extraordinary work.

In the Margins of the Pages
The *Book of Kells* is an illuminated manuscript of the gospels created in Ireland in 800 AD. It is on display at Trinity College, Dublin.

Around the Edges of the Pages
refers to the Holy Well at the foot of Glastonbury Tor, a place of legend and continuing pilgrimage.

Tapestries and Burgundy Trillium
Both poems refer to the "Lady and the Unicorn" tapestries hanging in Musée de Cluny, Musée National du Moyen Age in Paris. *A mon seul désir* is the name of one of them.

Histories
The illuminated manuscripts mentioned are part of an exhibit in the British Library in London. The *Lindisfarne Gospels* were created around 700 AD at the monastery of Lindisfarne off the coast of northeastern England. The *Rabula* Gospels are Syriac illuminated

manuscripts created during the sixth century. They are
part of the collection of Biblioteca Laurenziana in
Florence. Folding books are accordion style
illuminated manuscripts. The copy of one of the books
of the *Qur'an*, the sacred book of Islam in the exhibit,
was produced in Cairo in 1304.

Of That Country the Tongue
The italicized line is a quotation from "Two Trips to
Ireland" by David Young. The quote from Seamus
Heaney is from "Casting and
Gathering."

Family Stories in London
A Conversation With God, an exhibit of Icon
masterpieces from the Byzantine Museum of Athens,
was presented by the Embassy of Greece at the
Helenic Center in London in May, 1998. The name of
the Icon "Virgin Hodegetria" means "She Who Shows
the Way."

Inishmore
This is one of the Aran Islands that lie off the western
coast of Ireland. Part 1 is adapted from "Aran" by Irish
poet, Declan Collinge.

Cairns
The two italicized lines in Part 5 of are quoted from
"Matins" by Lynne Kuderko. The Italian *adumbrare*
means *to shadow*

Pilgrim
The art works referred to are painted by London artist Hérve Constant, *Coquille St. Jacques* and *Homage to Vincent*. The poem is dedicated to him. His shell series is a result of work he did at Santiago de Compostela which is the end of a route beginning at the French–Spanish border which has been walked by pilgrims for centuries. The shell worn around the neck is a symbol of the pilgrimage.

Making Form
The Book of Hours, *Tres Riche Heures du Duc de Berry* was painted by the Limbourg brothers beginning in 1413. The original can be seen at Musée Condé, Chantilly.

Translations
The story of Polycrates, a ruler of Samos in ancient Greece, was part of "De casibus virorum illustrium" written by Boccaccio in the fourteenth century. The illuminated manuscript described in the poem is on exhibit in the J. Paul Getty Museum in Los Angeles.

Learning in Normandy
The poem is dedicated to Anne-Marie Gautier in Avranches, Normandy. The monastery of Le Mont–Saint–Michel stands across the tide-bed from Avranches.

Closer to Flame
The thirteenth century stained glass windows of La Sainte–Chapelle in Paris are known for jewel tones of red and blue.

Learning in Normandy and **Learning How to Visit** were inspired by the work of Adam Zagajeweski.

The Name of Destination
One source of information about Hmong immigrants is *The Spirit Catches You and You Fall Down* by Anne Fadiman

Azotea
Fidesma Project is a school for children with special needs in San Antonio Ixtapa, Guatemala.

In the Middle
One thousand Quetzals equal approximately $120.00.

Hunger Well
The title phrase is from the book *Hunger Wall* by James Ragan.

Blue Moon
is dedicated to artist Merlyn Chesterman of Hartland, Devon.

Author

Mary Kay Rummel is the author of *Green Journey, Red Bird* published by Loonfeather Press. Her first poetry book, *This Body She's Entered,* was published by New Rivers Press as a Minnesota Voices Award winner and a poetry chapbook, *The Long Road Into North* was published by Juniper Press. She has had poems published in numerous literary journals and anthologies, most recently in, *ArtLife, Nimrod, Northeast,* and *Water-Stone Review.* Other publications include *Great River Review, Alaska Quarterly Review, Luna, Bloomsbury Review, California Quarterly, Flyway Literary Review, Abraxis* and *Passages North.* She was included in *33 Minnesota Poets* published by Nodin Press and was a winner of a Lake Superior Writers Award. In 2004 Andrew Motion, poet Laureate of England, chose a series of her poems to be exhibited at LondonArt. One of her poems was short listed for the 2004 Féile Filíochta International Poetry Competition in Dublin. She has performed her poetry with musicians and dancers. She has received fellowships for residencies at Vermont Studio Center (where many of the poems in this book were written), the Anderson Center and Norcroft. Mary Kay has published three books of nonfiction with Elizabeth Quintero. She is professor emeritus at the University of Minnesota, Duluth, currently teaches at California State University, Channel Islands and divides her time between California and Minnesota.

Visual Artist
Colleen McCallion is an artist from California currently living on an island off the coast of Boston and planning to return to France. She is eternally grateful for her artist residencies at the Vermont Studio Center where she met Mary Kay Rummel and produced the pastel (*Blue: Departing*—44 by 54 inches) for this cover.

Graphic Artist
Sandra Rummel is sister-in-law to the author. She transitioned easily from art teacher to graphic designer when she began her family. Today she divides her time between her husband Jim, her communications consulting practice, school board work and a commitment to environmental issues.

Printed in the United States
55165LVS00006B/289-309

9 781933 456379